HAL LEONARD EASY POP CHRISTMAS RHYTHMS

GUITAR METHOD

Supplement to Any Guitar Method

ISBN: 978-1-5400-2952-2

Contact Us:
Hal Leonard
7777 West Bluemound Road
Milwaukee, WI 53213
Email: info@halleonard.com

In Europe contact:
Hal Leonard Europe Limited
Distribution Centre, Newmarket Road
Bury St Edmunds, Suffolk, IP33 3YB
Email: info@halleonardeurope.com

In Australia contact:
Hal Leonard Australia Pty. Ltd.
4 Lentara Court
Cheltenham, Victoria, 3192 Australia
Email: info@halleonard.com.au

CONTENTS

SONG	CHORDS	PAGE
AWAY IN A MANGER	G, C, D7	6
SILVER BELLS	G, C, D7	8
SILENT NIGHT	G, D7, C	7
UP ON THE HOUSETOP	G, C, D7	10
I SAW THREE SHIPS	G, D	11
THE LITTLE DRUMMER BOY	G, D, C	12
THE STAR CAROL (CANZONE D'I ZAMPOGNARI)	G, D, D7	14
FELIZ NAVIDAD	G, A7, D	16
JOY TO THE WORLD	D, A7, G	18
JINGLE BELLS	G, C, D7, A7	20
C-H-R-I-S-T-M-A-S	G, C, D7, Em, A7	22
DECK THE HALL	G, D7, Em, A7, C	19
NUTTIN' FOR CHRISTMAS	G, C, A7, D7, Em	24
JOLLY OLD ST. NICHOLAS	G, D7, Em, G7, C, A7	26
O COME, ALL YE FAITHFUL	G, D, C, Em, A7, D7	27
STRUM PATTERNS & CHORDS		28

INTRODUCTION

Welcome to *Easy Pop Christmas Rhythms*, a collection of 15 favorites arranged for easy guitar chord strumming. If you're a beginning guitarist, you've come to the right place. With the songs in this book, you can practice basic chords and strumming patterns—plus learn how to play 15 great tunes!

This book can be used on its own or as a supplement to any guitar method. If you're using it along with the *Hal Leonard Guitar Method*, it coordinates with the skills introduced in Book 1. Use the table of contents on page 3 to see what chords each song contains and to determine when you're ready to play a song.

USING THE AUDIO

This product is available as a book/audio package so you can practice strumming along with a real band. Each song begins with a measure of clicks (or a partial measure, if the song begins with a pickup), which sets the tempo of the song and prepares you for playing along. You may want to practice each song on your own before playing it along with the audio.

SONG STRUCTURE

The songs in this book have different sections, which may or may not include the following:

Intro
This is usually a short instrumental section that "introduces" the song at the beginning.

Verse
This is one of the main sections of a song and conveys most of the storyline. A song usually has several verses, all with the same music but each with different lyrics.

Chorus
This is often the most memorable section of a song. Unlike the verse, the chorus usually has the same lyrics every time it repeats.

Bridge
This section is a break from the rest of the song, often having a very different chord progression and feel.

Solo
This is an instrumental section, often played over the verse or chorus structure.

Outro
Similar to an intro, this section brings the song to an end.

ENDINGS & REPEATS

Many of the songs have some new symbols that you must understand before playing. Each of these represents a different type of ending.

1st and 2nd Endings
These are indicated by brackets and numbers. The first time through a song section, play the first ending and then repeat. The second time through, skip the first ending, and play through the second ending.

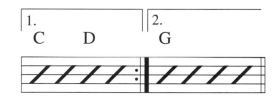

D.S.
This means "Dal Segno" or "from the sign." When you see this abbreviation above the staff, find the sign (𝄋) earlier in the song and resume playing from that point.

al Coda
This means "to the Coda," a concluding section in the song. If you see the words "D.S. al Coda," return to the sign (𝄋) earlier in the song and play until you see the words "To Coda," then skip to the Coda at the end of the song, indicated by the symbol: ⊕.

al Fine
This means "to the end." If you see the words "D.S. al Fine," return to the sign (𝄋) earlier in the song and play until you see the word "Fine."

D.C.
This means "Da Capo" or "from the head." When you see this abbreviation above the staff, return to the beginning (or "head") of the song and resume playing.

Away in a Manger

Words by John T. McFarland (v.3)
Music by James R. Murray

Verse
Moderately

1. A - way in a man - ger, no crib for a bed, the
cat - tle are low - ing, the ba - by a - wakes, but
near me, Lord Je - sus, I ask Thee to stay close

lit - tle Lord Je - sus laid down His sweet head. The
lit - tle Lord Je - sus, no cry - ing He makes. I
by me for - ev - er and love me, I pray. Bless

stars in the sky ____ looked down where He lay. The
love thee, Lord Je - sus, look down from the sky, and
all the dear chil - dren in Thy ten - der care and

lit - tle Lord Je - sus, a - sleep on the hay. 2. The
stay by my cra - dle 'til morn - ing is nigh. 3. Be
fit us for heav - en to live with Thee

there.

SILENT NIGHT

Words by Joseph Mohr
Translated by John F. Young
Music by Franz X. Gruber

Verse
Moderately

1. Si - lent night, ho - ly night, all is
2. Si - lent night, ho - ly night, shep - herds
3. *See additional lyrics*

calm, all is bright, 'round yon Vir - gin
quake at the sight. Glo - ries stream __ from

Moth - er and Child, Ho - ly In - fant so ten - der and
heav - en a - far, heav'n - ly hosts __ sing Al - le - lu -

mild, sleep in heav - en - ly peace. _____
ia; Christ the Sav - ior is born. _____

1., 2.

Sleep __ in heav - en - ly peace. _____
Christ __ the Sav - ior is born. _____

3.

birth. _____

Additional Lyrics

3. Silent night, holy night,
   Son of God, love's pure light.
   Radiant beams from thy holy face
   With the dawn of redeeming grace,
   Jesus Lord at Thy birth.
   Jesus Lord at Thy birth.

7

SILVER BELLS

from the Paramount Picture THE LEMON DROP KID

Words and Music by
Jay Livingston and Ray Evans

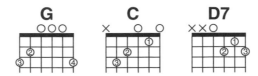

Verse

Moderately

1. Cit - y side - walks, bus - y side - walks dressed in
(2.) street - lights, e - ven stop - lights blink a

hol - i - day style, in the air there's a feel - ing of
bright red and green, as the shop - pers rush home with their

Christ - mas. Chil - dren laugh - ing, peo - ple pass - ing, meet - ing
treas - ures. Hear the snow crunch, see the kids bunch, this is

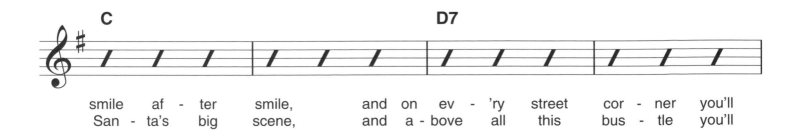

smile af - ter smile, and on ev - 'ry street cor - ner you'll
San - ta's big scene, and a - bove all this bus - tle you'll

Chorus

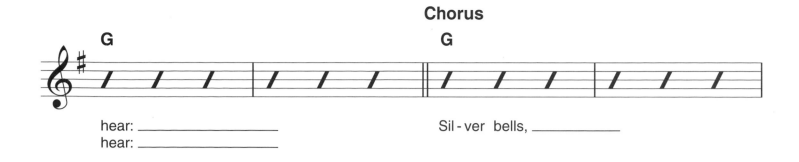

hear: _____
hear: _____

Sil - ver bells, _____

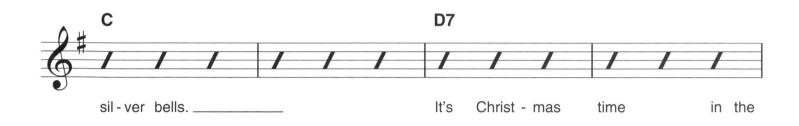

sil - ver bells. _____

It's Christ - mas time in the

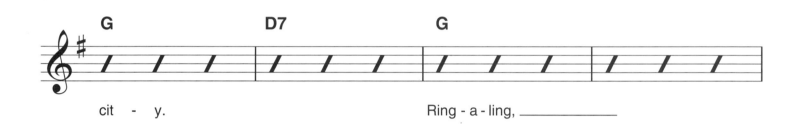

cit - y.

Ring - a - ling, _____

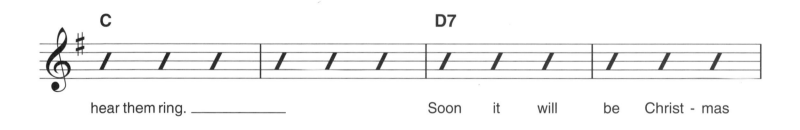

hear them ring. _____

Soon it will be Christ - mas

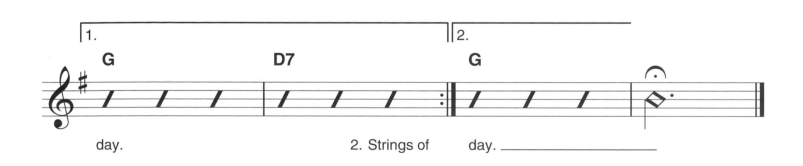

day.

2. Strings of day. _____

UP ON THE HOUSETOP

Words and Music by B.R. Hanby

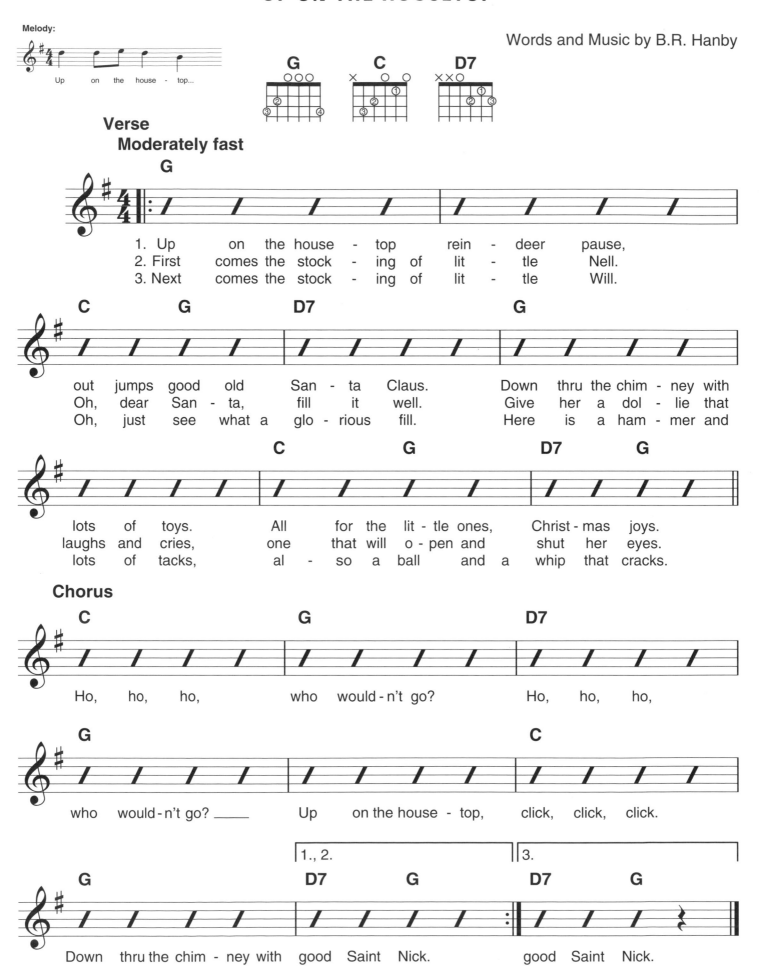

I SAW THREE SHIPS

Traditional English Carol

Melody:

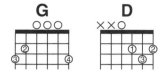

Verse
Moderately, in 2

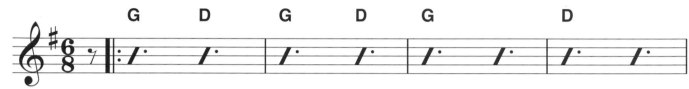

1. I saw three ships come sail - ing in, on Christ-mas Day, on Christ-mas Day; I
what was in those ships, all three, on Christ-mas Day, on Christ-mas Day; and
Vir - gin Mar-y and Christ were there, on Christ-mas Day, on Christ-mas Day; the
4., 5., 6. *See additional lyrics*

saw three ships come sail - ing in, on Christ-mas Day in the morn-ing. 2. And morn-ing.
what was in those ships, all three, on Christ-mas Day in the morn-ing? 3. The
Vir - gin Mar-y and Christ were there, on Christ-mas Day in the morn-ing.

Additional Lyrics

4. Pray, whither sailed those ships all three?
   On Christmas Day, on Christmas Day,
   Pray whither sailed those ships all three
   On Christmas Day in the morning?

5. Oh, they sailed into Bethlehem,
   On Christmas Day, on Christmas Day,
   Oh, they sailed into Bethlehem
   On Christmas Day in the morning.

6. And all the bells on earth shall ring,
   On Christmas Day, on Christmas Day,
   And all the bells on earth shall ring
   On Christmas Day in the morning.

THE LITTLE DRUMMER BOY

Words and Music by Harry Simeone,
Henry Onorati and Katherine Davis

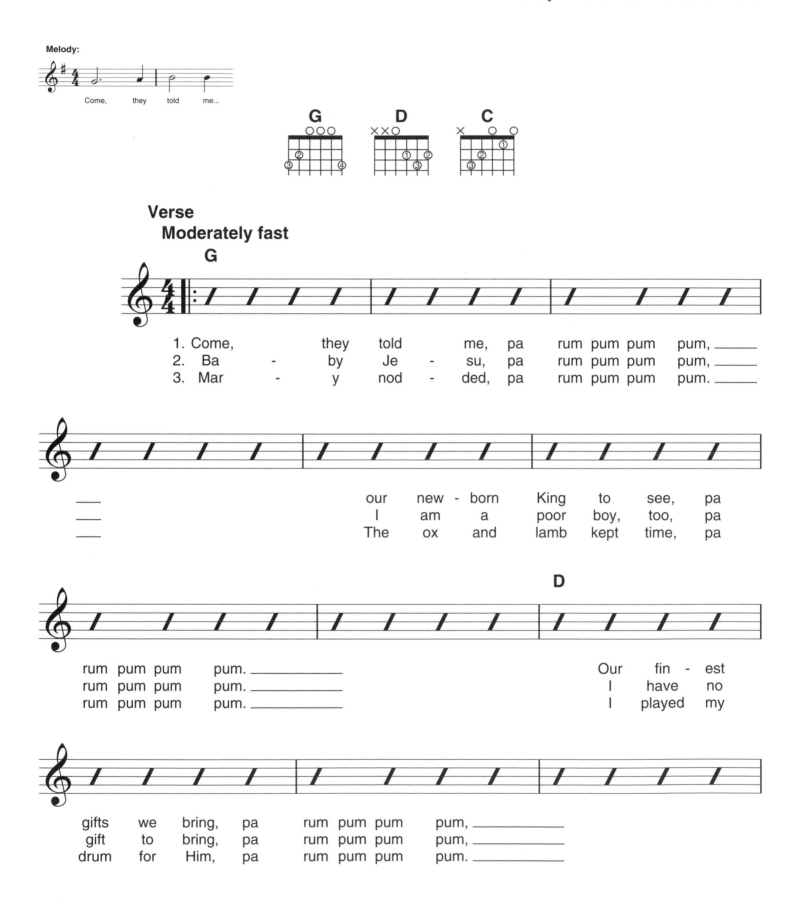

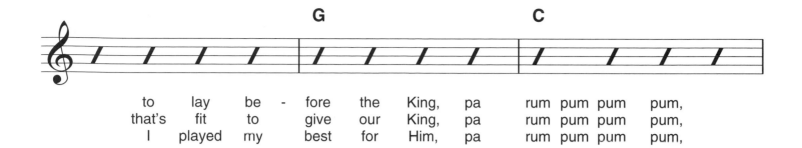

	G			C	
to	lay	be - fore the	King, pa	rum pum pum	pum,
that's	fit	to	give our	King, pa	rum pum pum	pum,
I	played	my	best for	Him, pa	rum pum pum	pum,

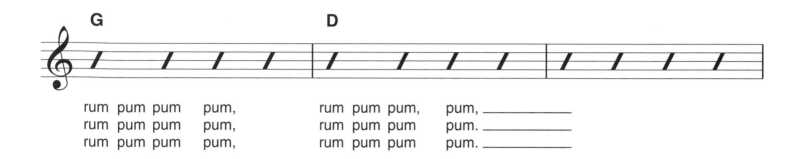

G		D		
rum pum pum	pum,	rum pum pum,	pum, _____
rum pum pum	pum,	rum pum pum	pum. _____
rum pum pum	pum,	rum pum pum	pum. _____

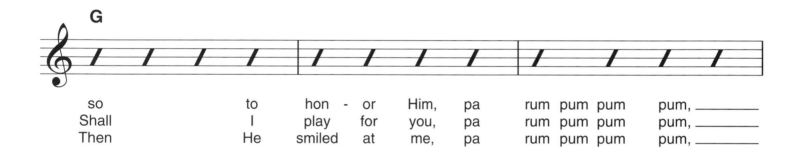

G				
so	to	hon - or Him, pa	rum pum pum	pum, _____
Shall	I	play for you, pa	rum pum pum	pum, _____
Then	He	smiled at me, pa	rum pum pum	pum, _____

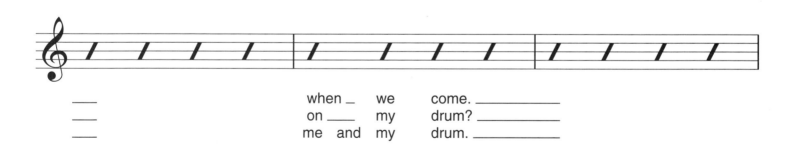

___	when _ we come. _____
___	on _ my drum? _____
___	me and my drum. _____

1., 2.   3.

THE STAR CAROL
(Canzone D'i Zampognari)

English Lyric and Music Adaptation by Peter Seeger
(Based on a Traditional Neapolitan Carol)

Melody:

'Twas   on   a   night...

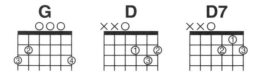

%. Verse
Moderately fast

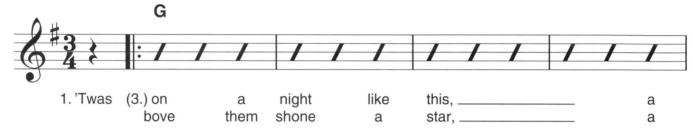

1. 'Twas (3.) on   a   night   like   this, _____   a   a
   bove   them   shone   a   star, _____   a

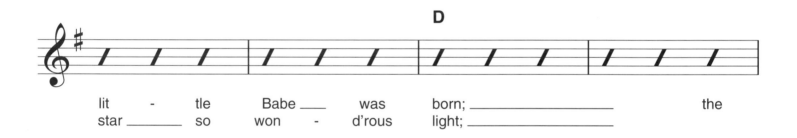

lit - tle   Babe ____   was   born; _____   the
star ____   so   won - d'rous   light; _____   the

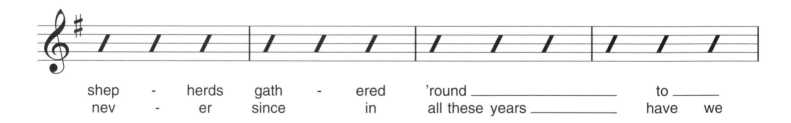

shep - herds   gath - ered   'round _____   to _____
nev - er   since   in   all these years _____   have   we

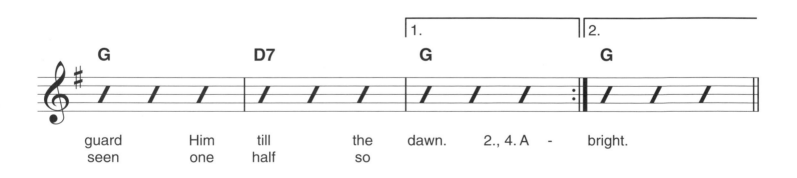

guard   Him   till   the   dawn.   2., 4. A - bright.
seen   one   half   so

Chorus

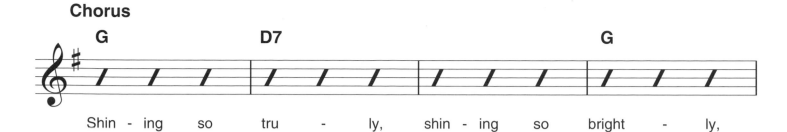

Shin - ing so tru - ly, shin - ing so bright - ly,

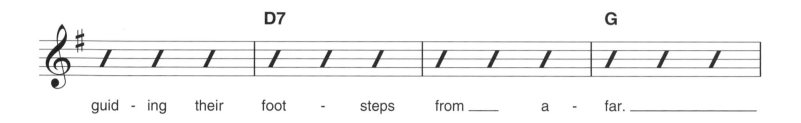

guid - ing their foot - steps from ___ a - far. _____

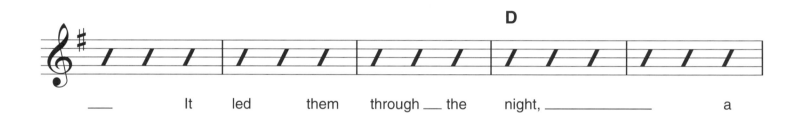

___ It led them through ___ the night, _____ a

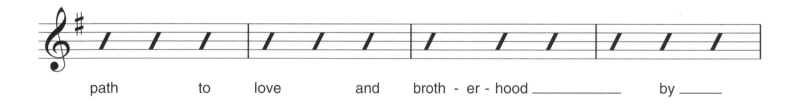

path to love and broth - er - hood _____ by _____

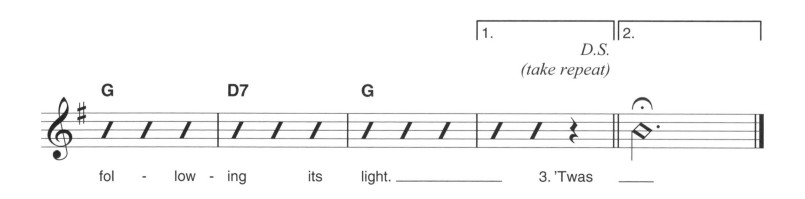

1. 2.
D.S.
(take repeat)

fol - low - ing its light. _____ 3. 'Twas ___

FELIZ NAVIDAD

Music and Lyrics by José Feliciano

Melody:

Fe - liz Na - vi - dad...

G A7 D

Moderately fast

%. Chorus

Fe - liz Na - vi - dad. Fe - liz Na - vi -

dad. Fe - liz Na - vi - dad. Pros - pe - ro a -

To Coda ⊕

- ño y fe - li - ci - dad. _____

1., 3. | 2.

N.C. N.C.

Fe - liz Na - vi - 1. I want to wish you a

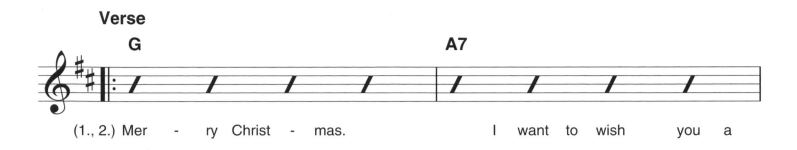

Verse

(1., 2.) Mer - ry Christ - mas.   I want to wish you a

Mer - ry Christ - mas.   I want to wish you a

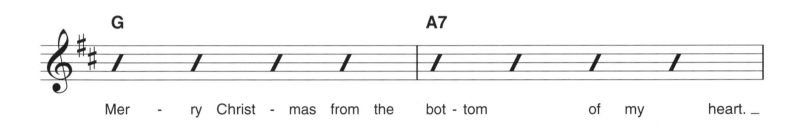

Mer - ry Christ - mas from the bot - tom of my heart. __

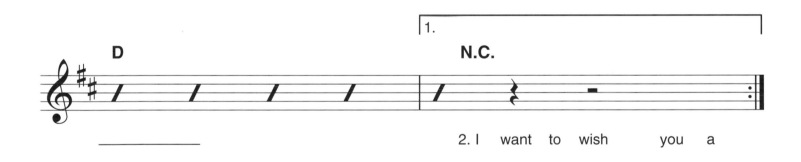

1.

_____   2. I want to wish you a

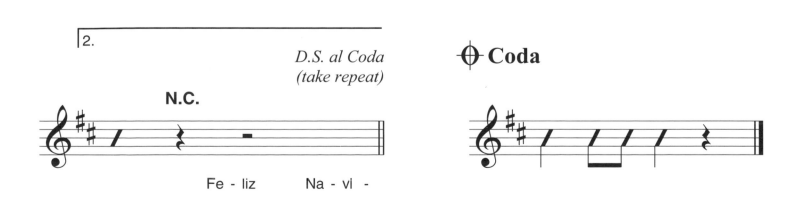

2.

D.S. al Coda
(take repeat)

Fe - liz Na - vi -

Coda

JOY TO THE WORLD

Words by Isaac Watts
Music by George Frideric Handel
Adapted by Lowell Mason

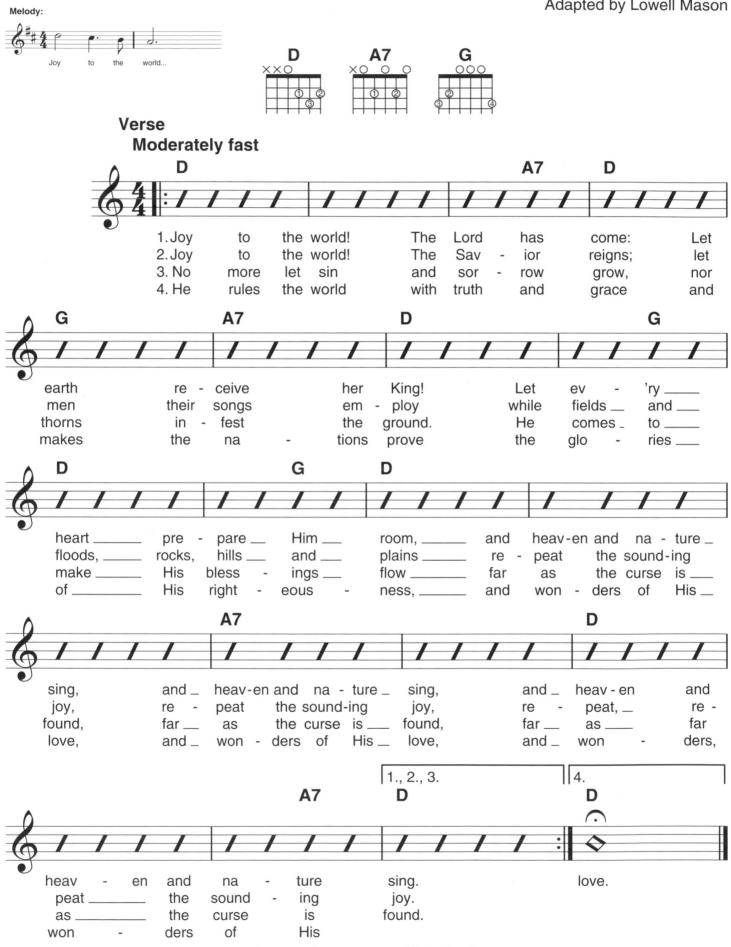

DECK THE HALL

Traditional Welsh Carol

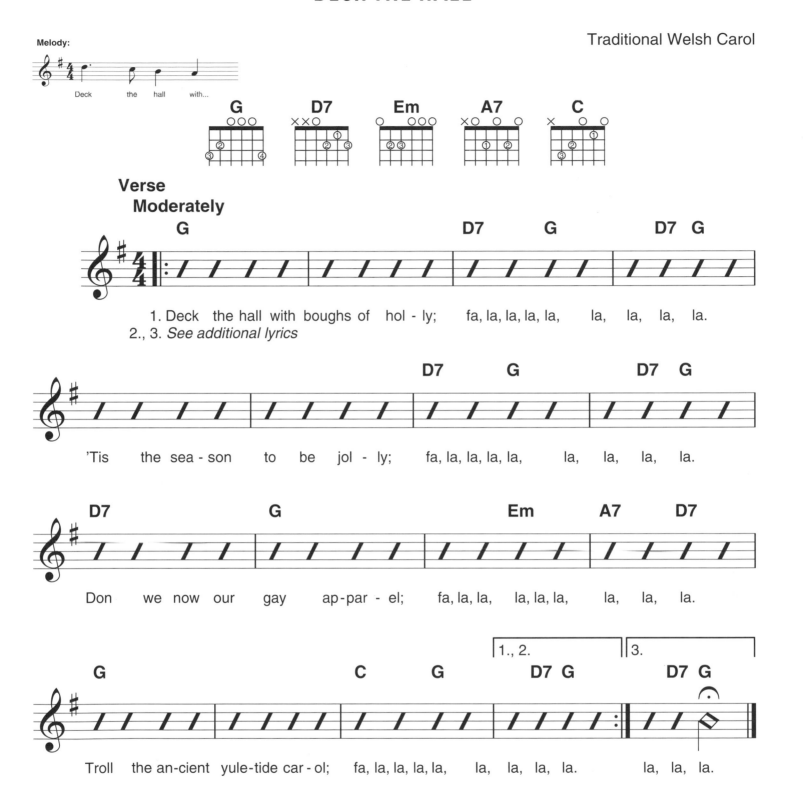

Verse
Moderately

1. Deck the hall with boughs of hol - ly;   fa, la, la, la, la,   la, la, la, la.
2., 3. *See additional lyrics*

'Tis   the sea - son   to be jol - ly;   fa, la, la, la, la,   la, la, la, la.

Don   we now our   gay   ap-par - el;   fa, la, la,   la, la, la,   la, la, la.

Troll   the an-cient yule-tide car - ol;   fa, la, la, la, la,   la, la, la, la.   la, la, la.

Additional Lyrics

2. See the blazing yule before us;
   Fa, la, la, la, la, la, la, la, la.
   Strike the harp and join the chorus;
   Fa, la, la, la, la, la, la, la, la.
   Follow me in merry measure;
   Fa, la, la, la, la, la, la, la.
   While I tell of Yuletide treasure,
   Fa, la, la, la, la, la, la, la, la.

3. Fast away the old year passes;
   Fa, la, la, la, la, la, la, la, la.
   Hail the new ye lads and lasses;
   Fa, la, la, la, la, la, la, la, la.
   Sing we joyous, all together;
   Fa, la, la, la, la, la, la, la, la.
   Heedless of the wind and weather;
   Fa, la, la, la, la, la, la, la, la.

JINGLE BELLS

Words and Music by J. Pierpont

Chorus

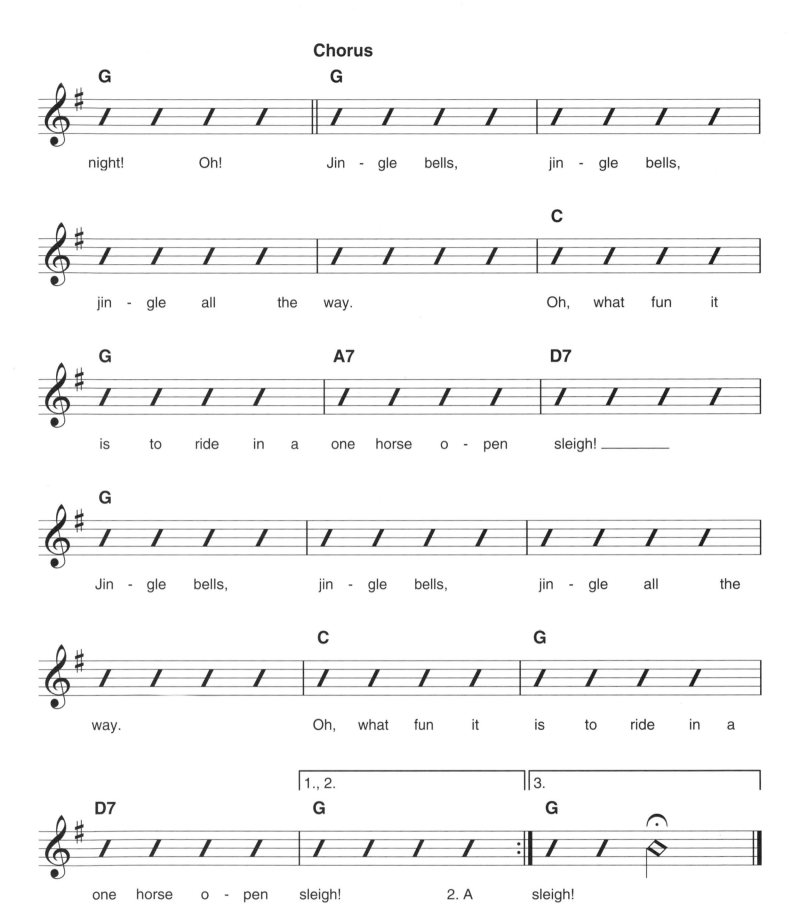

night! Oh! Jin - gle bells, jin - gle bells,

jin - gle all the way. Oh, what fun it

is to ride in a one horse o - pen sleigh! _____

Jin - gle bells, jin - gle bells, jin - gle all the

way. Oh, what fun it is to ride in a

one horse o - pen sleigh! 2. A sleigh!

Additional Lyrics

2. A day or two ago, I thought I'd take a ride,
   And soon Miss Fannie Bright was sitting by my side.
   The horse was lean and lank,
   Misfortune seemed his lot.
   He got into a drifted bank and we, we got upshot! Oh!

3. Now the ground is white, go it while you're young.
   Take the girls tonight and sing this sleighing song.
   Just get a bobtail bay,
   Two-forty for his speed.
   Then hitch him to an open sleigh and
   Crack, you'll take the lead! Oh!

C-H-R-I-S-T-M-A-S

Words by Jenny Lou Carson
Music by Eddy Arnold

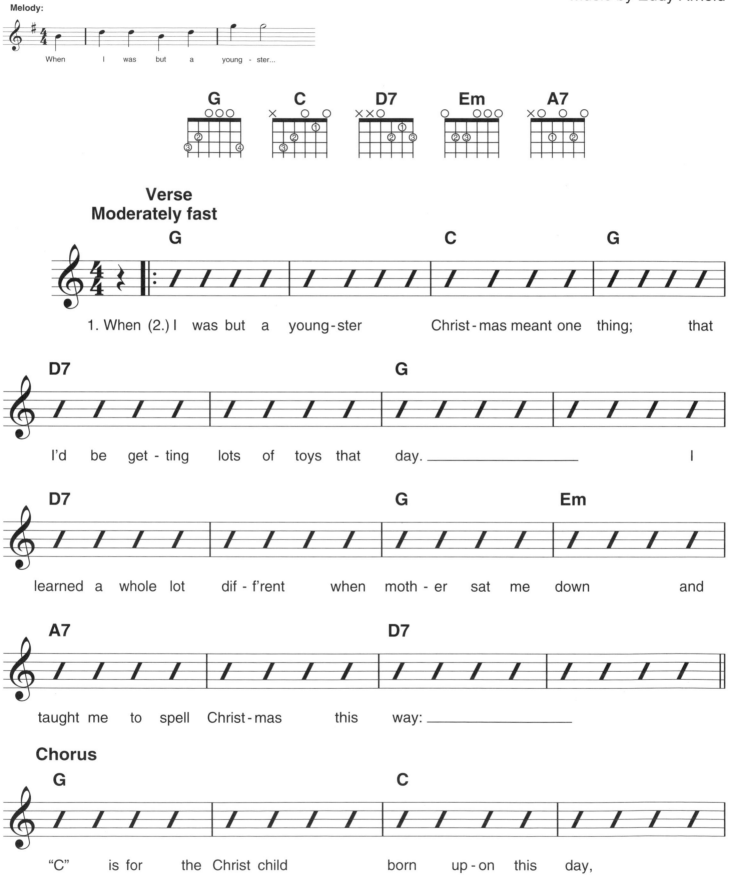

Melody:

When I was but a young-ster...

G   C   D7   Em   A7

Verse
Moderately fast

G   C   G

1. When (2.) I was but a young-ster   Christ-mas meant one thing;   that

D7   G

I'd be get-ting lots of toys that day. _____ I

D7   G   Em

learned a whole lot dif-f'rent when moth-er sat me down and

A7   D7

taught me to spell Christ-mas this way: _____

Chorus
G   C

"C" is for the Christ child born up-on this day,

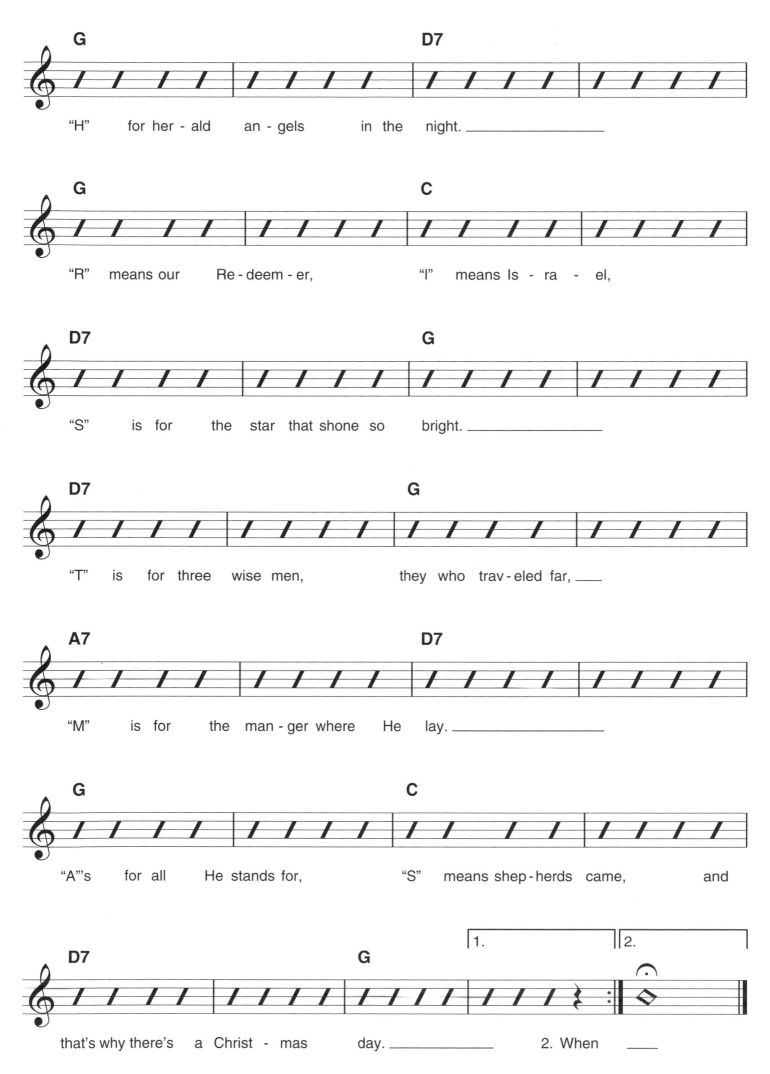

NUTTIN' FOR CHRISTMAS

Words and Music by Roy C. Bennett
and Sid Tepper

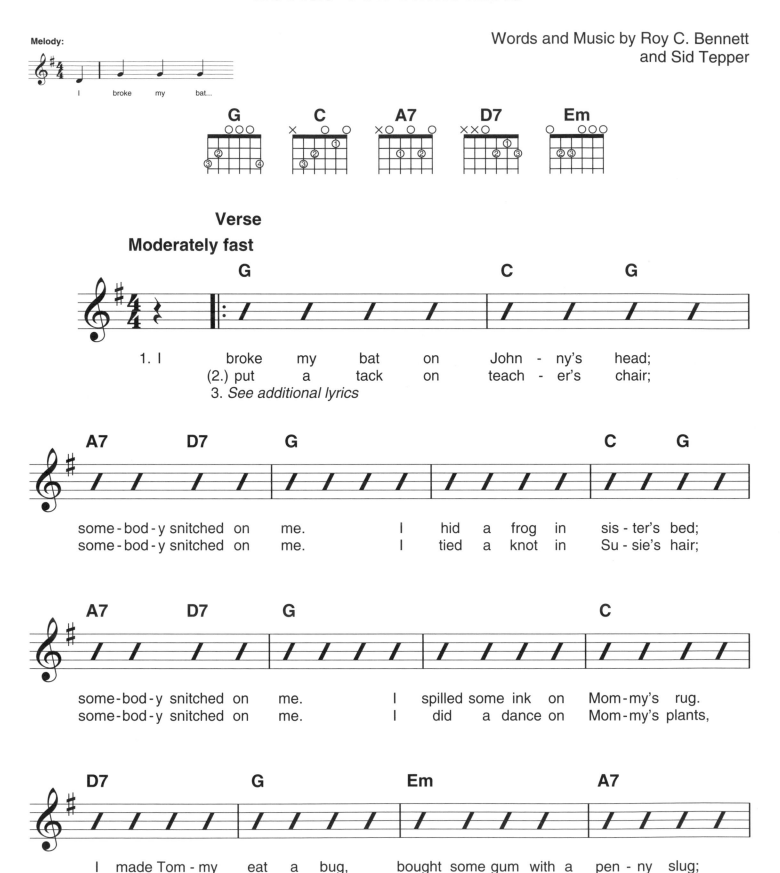

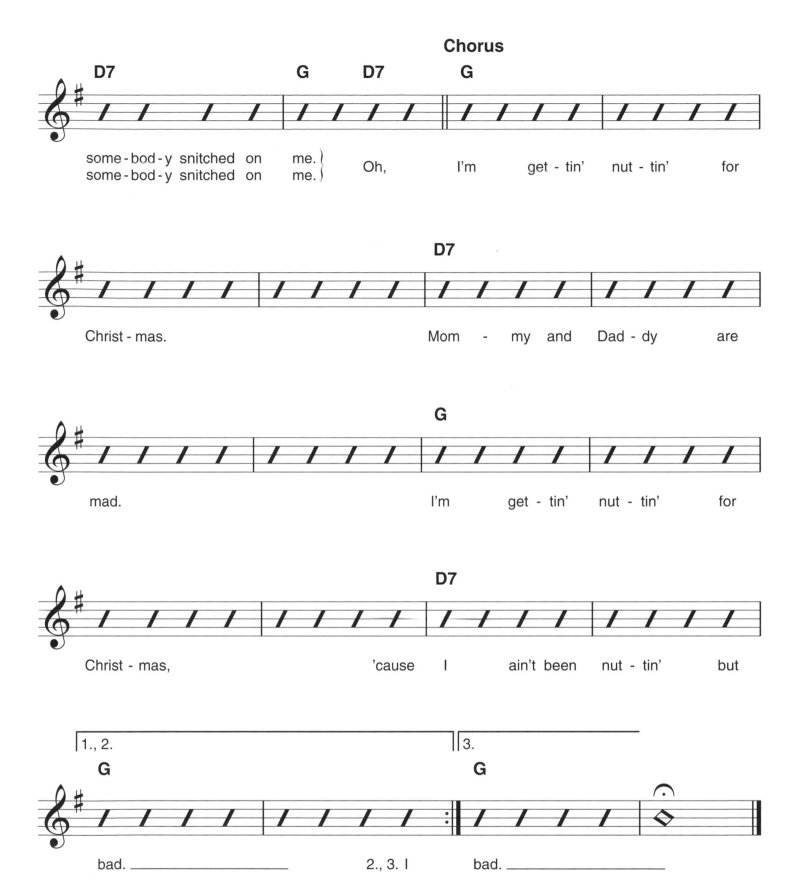

Additional Lyrics

3. I won't be seeing Santa Claus;
   Somebody snitched on me.
   He won't come visit me because
   Somebody snitched on me.
   Next year, I'll be going straight.
   Next year, I'll be good, just wait.
   I'd start now but it's too late;
   Somebody snitched on me.

JOLLY OLD ST. NICHOLAS

Traditional 19th Century American Carol

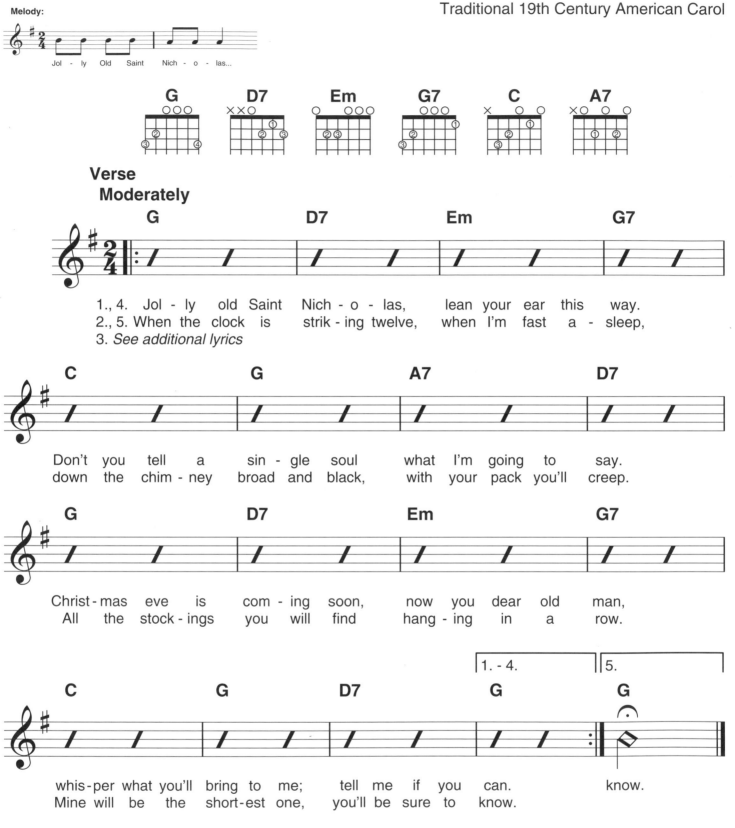

Verse
Moderately

1., 4. Jol - ly old Saint Nich - o - las, lean your ear this way.
2., 5. When the clock is strik - ing twelve, when I'm fast a - sleep,
3. *See additional lyrics*

Don't you tell a sin - gle soul what I'm going to say.
down the chim - ney broad and black, with your pack you'll creep.

Christ - mas eve is com - ing soon, now you dear old man,
All the stock - ings you will find hang - ing in a row.

whis - per what you'll bring to me; tell me if you can. know.
Mine will be the short - est one, you'll be sure to know.

Additional Lyrics

3. Johnny wants a pair of skates; Susy wants a sled.
   Nellie wants a picture book, yellow, blue and red.
   Now I think I'll leave to you what to give the rest.
   Choose for me, dear Santa Claus.
   You will know the best.

O COME, ALL YE FAITHFUL

Music by John Francis Wade
Latin Words translated by Frederick Oakeley

STRUM PATTERNS

The first responsibility of a chord player is to *play the right chord on time*. Keep this in mind as you learn new strumming patterns. No matter how concerned you might be with right-hand strumming, getting to the correct chord with your left hand is more important. If necessary, leave the old chord early in order to arrive at the new chord on time.

That said, here are some suggested strum patterns. Choose one that challenges you, and practice it. Whenever you learn a new chord or progression, try putting it into one of these patterns. Also, try applying these to the songs in this book.

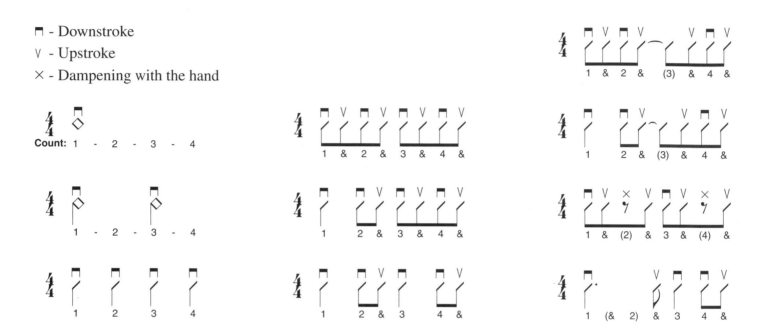

Eighth notes in the above strums may be played even or uneven ("swung") depending on the style of music.

CHORDS

Here are all the chords needed to play the songs in this book.

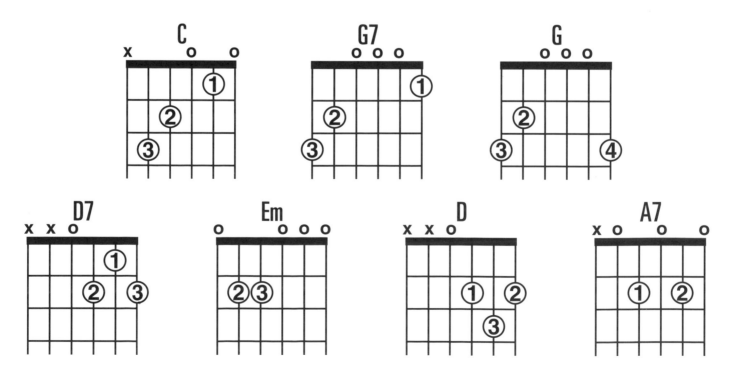

These are presented in the order you learned them in Book 1 of the *Hal Leonard Guitar Method*.

HAL LEONARD GUITAR METHOD
by Will Schmid and Greg Koch

THE HAL LEONARD GUITAR METHOD is designed for anyone just learning to play acoustic or electric guitar. It is based on years of teaching guitar students of all ages, and it also reflects some of the best guitar teaching ideas from around the world. This comprehensive method includes: A learning sequence carefully paced with clear instructions; popular songs which increase the incentive to learn to play; versatility – can be used as self-instruction or with a teacher; audio accompaniments so that students have fun and sound great while practicing.

BOOK 1
00699010 Book $8.99
00699027 Book with audio on CD & Online $12.99
00155480 Deluxe Beginner Pack
(Book/DVD/CD/Online Audio &
Video/Poster) $19.99

BOOK 2
00699020 Book $8.99
00697313 Book/CD Pack $12.99

BOOK 3
00699030 Book $8.99
00697316 Book/Online Audio...............................$12.99

COMPOSITE
Books 1, 2, and 3 bound together in an easy-to-use spiral binding.
00699040 Books Only $16.99
00697342 Book/Online Audio...............................$24.99

DVD
FOR THE BEGINNING ELECTRIC
OR ACOUSTIC GUITARIST
00697318 DVD $19.95
00697341 Book/CD Pack and DVD $24.99

GUITAR FOR KIDS
A BEGINNER'S GUIDE WITH STEP-BY-STEP INSTRUCTION
FOR ACOUSTIC AND ELECTRIC GUITAR
by Bob Morris and Jeff Schroedl
00865003 Book 1 – Book/Online Audio $12.99
00697402 Songbook Book/Online Audio.................$9.99
00128437 Book 2 – Book/Online Audio $12.99

SONGBOOKS

EASY POP MELODIES
00697281 Book $6.99
00697440 Book/Online Audio...............................$14.99

MORE EASY POP MELODIES
00697280 Book $6.99
00697269 Book/Online Audio...............................$14.99

EVEN MORE EASY POP MELODIES
00699154 Book $6.99
00697439 Book/Online Audio...............................$14.99

EASY POP RHYTHMS
00697336 Book $7.99
00697441 Book/Online Audio...............................$14.99

MORE EASY POP RHYTHMS
00697338 Book $7.99
00697322 Book/Online Audio...............................$14.99

EVEN MORE EASY POP RHYTHMS
00697340 Book $7.99
00697323 Book/Online Audio...............................$14.99

EASY SOLO GUITAR PIECES
00110407 Book $9.99

EASY POP CHRISTMAS MELODIES
00697417 Book $6.99
00697416 Book/Online Audio...............................$14.99

EASY POP CHRISTMAS RHYTHMS
00278177 Book $6.99
00278175 Book/Online Audio...............................$14.99

LEAD LICKS
00697345 Book/Online Audio...............................$10.99

RHYTHM RIFFS
00697346 Book/Online Audio...............................$10.99

STYLISTIC METHODS

ACOUSTIC GUITAR
00697347 Book/Online Audio...............................$16.99
00237969 Acoustic Guitar Songs
(with Online Audio)................................$16.99

BLUEGRASS GUITAR
00697405 Book/Online Audio...............................$16.99

BLUES GUITAR
00697326 Book/Online Audio...............................$16.99
00697385 Blues Guitar Songs
(with Online Audio)................................$14.99

BRAZILIAN GUITAR
00697415 Book/Online Audio...............................$14.99

CHRISTIAN GUITAR
00695947 Book/Online Audio...............................$12.99
00697408 Christian Guitar Songs.........................$14.99

CLASSICAL GUITAR
00697376 Book/Online Audio...............................$15.99
00697388 Classical Guitar Pieces.........................$9.99

COUNTRY GUITAR
00697337 Book/Online Audio...............................$22.99
00697400 Country Guitar Songs $16.99

FINGERSTYLE GUITAR
00697378 Book/Online Audio...............................$19.99
00697432 Fingergstyle Guitar Songs
(with Online Audio)................................$14.99

FLAMENCO GUITAR
00697363 Book/Online Audio...............................$15.99

FOLK GUITAR
00697414 Book/Online Audio...............................$14.99

JAZZ GUITAR
00695359 Book/Online Audio...............................$19.99
00697386 Jazz Guitar Songs $14.95

JAZZ-ROCK FUSION
00697387 Book/Online Audio...............................$19.99

ROCK GUITAR
00697319 Book/Online Audio...............................$16.99
00697383 Rock Guitar Songs $14.95

ROCKABILLY GUITAR
00697407 Book/Online Audio...............................$16.99

R&B GUITAR
00697356 Book/CD Pack $16.99
00697433 R&B Guitar Songs...............................$14.99

TENOR GUITAR
00148330 Book/Online Audio...............................$12.99

REFERENCE

ARPEGGIO FINDER
00697351 9" x 12" Edition $6.99

INCREDIBLE CHORD FINDER
00697200 6" x 9" Edition $6.99
00697208 9" x 12" Edition $6.99

INCREDIBLE SCALE FINDER
00695568 6" x 9" Edition $5.99
00695490 9" x 12" Edition $6.99

GUITAR CHORD, SCALE & ARPEGGIO FINDER
00697410 ....$19.99

GUITAR SETUP & MAINTENANCE
00697427 6" x 9" Edition $14.99
00697421 9" x 12" Edition $12.99

GUITAR TECHNIQUES
00697389 Book/CD Pack $14.99

GUITAR PRACTICE PLANNER
00697401..$5.99

MUSIC THEORY FOR GUITARISTS
00695790 Book/Online Audio...............................$19.99

HAL•LEONARD®

www.halleonard.com

Prices, contents and availability subject to change without notice.

0618

EASY GUITAR WITH NOTES & TAB

This series features simplified arrangements with notes, tab, chord charts, and strum and pick patterns.

MIXED FOLIOS

00702287	Acoustic	$16.99
00702002	Acoustic Rock Hits for Easy Guitar	$14.99
00702166	All-Time Best Guitar Collection	$19.99
00699665	Beatles Best	$14.99
00702232	Best Acoustic Songs for Easy Guitar	$14.99
00119835	Best Children's Songs	$16.99
00702233	Best Hard Rock Songs	$14.99
00703055	The Big Book of Nursery Rhymes & Children's Songs	$14.99
00322179	The Big Easy Book of Classic Rock Guitar	$24.95
00698978	Big Christmas Collection	$17.99
00702394	Bluegrass Songs for Easy Guitar	$12.99
00703387	Celtic Classics	$14.99
00224808	Chart Hits of 2016-2017	$14.99
00702149	Children's Christian Songbook	$9.99
00702237	Christian Acoustic Favorites	$12.95
00702028	Christmas Classics	$8.99
00101779	Christmas Guitar	$14.99
00702185	Christmas Hits	$9.95
00702141	Classic Rock	$8.95
00702203	CMT's 100 Greatest Country Songs	$27.95
00702283	The Contemporary Christian Collection	$16.99

00702239	Country Classics for Easy Guitar	$19.99
00702282	Country Hits of 2009–2010	$14.99
00702257	Easy Acoustic Guitar Songs	$14.99
00702280	Easy Guitar Tab White Pages	$29.99
00702041	Favorite Hymns for Easy Guitar	$10.99
00140841	4-Chord Hymns for Guitar	$7.99
00702281	4 Chord Rock	$10.99
00126894	Frozen	$14.99
00702286	Glee	$16.99
00699374	Gospel Favorites	$14.95
00122138	The Grammy Awards® Record of the Year 1958-2011	$19.99
00702160	The Great American Country Songbook	$16.99
00702050	Great Classical Themes for Easy Guitar	$8.99
00702116	Greatest Hymns for Guitar	$10.99
00702130	The Groovy Years	$9.95
00702184	Guitar Instrumentals	$9.95
00148030	Halloween Guitar Songs	$14.99
00702273	Irish Songs	$12.99
00702275	Jazz Favorites for Easy Guitar	$15.99
00702274	Jazz Standards for Easy Guitar	$15.99
00702162	Jumbo Easy Guitar Songbook	$19.99
00702258	Legends of Rock	$14.99
00702261	Modern Worship Hits	$14.99

00702189	MTV's 100 Greatest Pop Songs	$24.95
00702272	1950s Rock	$15.99
00702271	1960s Rock	$15.99
00702270	1970s Rock	$15.99
00702269	1980s Rock	$15.99
00702268	1990s Rock	$15.99
00109725	Once	$14.99
00702187	Selections from O Brother Where Art Thou?	$15.99
00702178	100 Songs for Kids	$14.99
00702515	Pirates of the Caribbean	$12.99
00702125	Praise and Worship for Guitar	$10.99
00702285	Southern Rock Hits	$12.99
00121535	30 Easy Celtic Guitar Solos	$14.99
00702220	Today's Country Hits	$9.95
00121900	Today's Women of Pop & Rock	$14.99
00702294	Top Worship Hits	$15.99
00702255	VH1's 100 Greatest Hard Rock Songs	$27.99
00702175	VH1's 100 Greatest Songs of Rock and Roll	$24.95
00702253	Wicked	$12.99

ARTIST COLLECTIONS

00702267	AC/DC for Easy Guitar	$15.99
00702598	Adele for Easy Guitar	$15.99
00702040	Best of the Allman Brothers	$15.99
00702865	J.S. Bach for Easy Guitar	$14.99
00702169	Best of The Beach Boys	$12.99
00702292	The Beatles — 1	$19.99
00125796	Best of Chuck Berry	$14.99
00702201	The Essential Black Sabbath	$12.95
02501615	Zac Brown Band — The Foundation	$16.99
02501621	Zac Brown Band — You Get What You Give	$16.99
00702043	Best of Johnny Cash	$16.99
00702263	Best of Casting Crowns	$14.99
00702090	Eric Clapton's Best	$10.95
00702086	Eric Clapton — from the Album Unplugged	$10.95
00702202	The Essential Eric Clapton	$14.99
00702250	blink-182 — Greatest Hits	$15.99
00702053	Best of Patsy Cline	$14.99
00702229	The Very Best of Creedence Clearwater Revival	$15.99
00702145	Best of Jim Croce	$15.99
00702278	Crosby, Stills & Nash	$12.99
00702219	David Crowder*Band Collection	$12.95
14042809	Bob Dylan	$14.99
00702276	Fleetwood Mac — Easy Guitar Collection	$14.99
00139462	The Very Best of Grateful Dead	$15.99
00702136	Best of Merle Haggard	$12.99
00702227	Jimi Hendrix — Smash Hits	$14.99
00702288	Best of Hillsong United	$12.99
00702236	Best of Antonio Carlos Jobim	$14.99

00702245	Elton John — Greatest Hits 1970–2002	$14.99
00129855	Jack Johnson	$15.99
00702204	Robert Johnson	$10.99
00702234	Selections from Toby Keith — 35 Biggest Hits	$12.95
00702003	Kiss	$10.99
00110578	Best of Kutless	$12.99
00702216	Lynyrd Skynyrd	$15.99
00702182	The Essential Bob Marley	$12.95
00146081	Maroon 5	$14.99
00121925	Bruno Mars – Unorthodox Jukebox	$12.99
00702248	Paul McCartney — All the Best	$14.99
00702129	Songs of Sarah McLachlan	$12.95
00125484	The Best of MercyMe	$12.99
02501316	Metallica — Death Magnetic	$19.99
00702209	Steve Miller Band — Young Hearts (Greatest Hits)	$12.95
00124167	Jason Mraz	$15.99
00702096	Best of Nirvana	$15.99
00702211	The Offspring — Greatest Hits	$12.95
00138026	One Direction	$14.99
00702030	Best of Roy Orbison	$14.99
00702144	Best of Ozzy Osbourne	$14.99
00702279	Tom Petty	$12.99
00102911	Pink Floyd	$16.99
00702139	Elvis Country Favorites	$14.99
00702293	The Very Best of Prince	$15.99
00699415	Best of Queen for Guitar	$14.99
00109279	Best of R.E.M.	$14.99
00702208	Red Hot Chili Peppers — Greatest Hits	$14.99

00198960	The Rolling Stones	$16.99
00174793	The Very Best of Santana	$14.99
00702196	Best of Bob Seger	$12.95
00146046	Ed Sheeran	$14.99
00702252	Frank Sinatra — Nothing But the Best	$12.99
00702010	Best of Rod Stewart	$16.99
00702049	Best of George Strait	$14.99
00702259	Taylor Swift for Easy Guitar	$15.99
00702260	Taylor Swift — Fearless	$14.99
00139727	Taylor Swift — 1989	$17.99
00115960	Taylor Swift — Red	$16.99
00253667	Taylor Swift — Reputation	$17.99
00702290	Taylor Swift — Speak Now	$15.99
00702226	Chris Tomlin — See the Morning	$12.95
00148643	Train	$14.99
00702427	U2 — 18 Singles	$16.99
00102711	Van Halen	$16.99
00702108	Best of Stevie Ray Vaughan	$14.99
00702123	Best of Hank Williams	$14.99
00702111	Stevie Wonder — Guitar Collection	$9.95
00702228	Neil Young — Greatest Hits	$15.99
00119133	Neil Young — Harvest	$14.99
00702188	Essential ZZ Top	$10.95

Prices, contents and availability subject to change without notice.

HAL•LEONARD®

Visit Hal Leonard online at
www.halleonard.com

0418

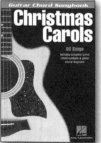

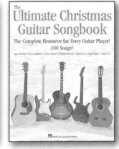

Hal•Leonard® GUITAR PLAY-ALONG

AUDIO ACCESS INCLUDED

This series will help you play your favorite songs quickly and easily. Just follow the tab and listen to the audio to the hear how the guitar should sound, and then play along using the separate backing tracks. Audio files also include software to slow down the tempo without changing pitch. The melody and lyrics are included in the book so that you can sing or simply follow along.

INCLUDES TAB

VOL. 1 – ROCK	00699570 / $16.99
VOL. 2 – ACOUSTIC	00699569 / $16.99
VOL. 3 – HARD ROCK	00699573 / $17.99
VOL. 4 – POP/ROCK	00699571 / $16.99
VOL. 6 – '90S ROCK	00699572 / $16.99
VOL. 7 – BLUES	00699575 / $17.99
VOL. 8 – ROCK	00699585 / $16.99
VOL. 9 – EASY ACOUSTIC SONGS	00151708 / $16.99
VOL. 10 – ACOUSTIC	00699586 / $16.95
VOL. 11 – EARLY ROCK	00699579 / $14.95
VOL. 12 – POP/ROCK	00699587 / $14.95
VOL. 13 – FOLK ROCK	00699581 / $16.99
VOL. 14 – BLUES ROCK	00699582 / $16.99
VOL. 15 – R&B	00699583 / $16.99
VOL. 16 – JAZZ	00699584 / $15.95
VOL. 17 – COUNTRY	00699588 / $16.99
VOL. 18 – ACOUSTIC ROCK	00699577 / $15.95
VOL. 19 – SOUL	00699578 / $15.99
VOL. 20 – ROCKABILLY	00699580 / $16.99
VOL. 21 – SANTANA	00174525 / $17.99
VOL. 22 – CHRISTMAS	00699600 / $15.99
VOL. 23 – SURF	00699635 / $15.99
VOL. 24 – ERIC CLAPTON	00699649 / $17.99
VOL. 25 – THE BEATLES	00198265 / $17.99
VOL. 26 – ELVIS PRESLEY	00699643 / $16.99
VOL. 27 – DAVID LEE ROTH	00699645 / $16.95
VOL. 28 – GREG KOCH	00699646 / $16.99
VOL. 29 – BOB SEGER	00699647 / $15.99
VOL. 30 – KISS	00699644 / $16.99
VOL. 32 – THE OFFSPRING	00699653 / $14.95
VOL. 33 – ACOUSTIC CLASSICS	00699656 / $17.99
VOL. 34 – CLASSIC ROCK	00699658 / $17.99
VOL. 35 – HAIR METAL	00699660 / $17.99
VOL. 36 – SOUTHERN ROCK	00699661 / $17.99
VOL. 37 – ACOUSTIC UNPLUGGED	00699662 / $22.99
VOL. 38 – BLUES	00699663 / $16.95
VOL. 39 – '80S METAL	00699664 / $16.99
VOL. 40 – INCUBUS	00699668 / $17.95
VOL. 41 – ERIC CLAPTON	00699669 / $17.99
VOL. 42 – COVER BAND HITS	00211597 / $16.99
VOL. 43 – LYNYRD SKYNYRD	00699681 / $17.95
VOL. 44 – JAZZ	00699689 / $16.99
VOL. 45 – TV THEMES	00699718 / $14.95
VOL. 46 – MAINSTREAM ROCK	00699722 / $16.95
VOL. 47 – HENDRIX SMASH HITS	00699723 / $19.99
VOL. 48 – AEROSMITH CLASSICS	00699724 / $17.99
VOL. 49 – STEVIE RAY VAUGHAN	00699725 / $17.99
VOL. 50 – VAN HALEN 1978-1984	00110269 / $17.99
VOL. 51 – ALTERNATIVE '90S	00699727 / $14.99
VOL. 52 – FUNK	00699728 / $15.99
VOL. 53 – DISCO	00699729 / $14.99
VOL. 54 – HEAVY METAL	00699730 / $15.99
VOL. 55 – POP METAL	00699731 / $14.95
VOL. 56 – FOO FIGHTERS	00699749 / $15.99
VOL. 59 – CHET ATKINS	00702347 / $16.99
VOL. 62 – CHRISTMAS CAROLS	00699798 / $12.95
VOL. 63 – CREEDENCE CLEARWATER REVIVAL	00699802 / $16.99
VOL. 64 – THE ULTIMATE OZZY OSBOURNE	00699803 / $17.99
VOL. 66 – THE ROLLING STONES	00699807 / $17.99
VOL. 67 – BLACK SABBATH	00699808 / $16.99
VOL. 68 – PINK FLOYD – DARK SIDE OF THE MOON	00699809 / $16.99

VOL. 69 – ACOUSTIC FAVORITES	00699810 / $16.99
VOL. 70 – OZZY OSBOURNE	00699805 / $16.99
VOL. 73 – BLUESY ROCK	00699829 / $16.99
VOL. 74 – SIMPLE STRUMMING SONGS	00151706 / $19.99
VOL. 75 – TOM PETTY	00699882 / $16.99
VOL. 76 – COUNTRY HITS	00699884 / $16.99
VOL. 77 – BLUEGRASS	00699910 / $15.99
VOL. 78 – NIRVANA	00700132 / $16.99
VOL. 79 – NEIL YOUNG	00700133 / $24.99
VOL. 80 – ACOUSTIC ANTHOLOGY	00700175 / $19.95
VOL. 81 – ROCK ANTHOLOGY	00700176 / $22.99
VOL. 82 – EASY SONGS	00700177 / $14.99
VOL. 83 – THREE CHORD SONGS	00700178 / $16.99
VOL. 84 – STEELY DAN	00700200 / $16.99
VOL. 85 – THE POLICE	00700269 / $16.99
VOL. 86 – BOSTON	00700465 / $16.99
VOL. 87 – ACOUSTIC WOMEN	00700763 / $14.99
VOL. 89 – REGGAE	00700468 / $15.99
VOL. 90 – CLASSICAL POP	00700469 / $14.99
VOL. 91 – BLUES INSTRUMENTALS	00700505 / $15.99
VOL. 92 – EARLY ROCK INSTRUMENTALS	00700506 / $15.99
VOL. 93 – ROCK INSTRUMENTALS	00700507 / $16.99
VOL. 94 – SLOW BLUES	00700508 / $16.99
VOL. 95 – BLUES CLASSICS	00700509 / $15.99
VOL. 96 – BEST COUNTRY HITS	00211615 / $16.99
VOL. 97 – CHRISTMAS CLASSICS	00236542 / $14.99
VOL. 99 – ZZ TOP	00700762 / $16.99
VOL. 100 – B.B. KING	00700466 / $16.99
VOL. 101 – SONGS FOR BEGINNERS	00701917 / $14.99
VOL. 102 – CLASSIC PUNK	00700769 / $14.99
VOL. 103 – SWITCHFOOT	00700773 / $16.99
VOL. 104 – DUANE ALLMAN	00700846 / $16.99
VOL. 105 – LATIN	00700939 / $16.99
VOL. 106 – WEEZER	00700958 / $14.99
VOL. 107 – CREAM	00701069 / $16.99
VOL. 108 – THE WHO	00701053 / $16.99
VOL. 109 – STEVE MILLER	00701054 / $17.99
VOL. 110 – SLIDE GUITAR HITS	00701055 / $16.99
VOL. 111 – JOHN MELLENCAMP	00701056 / $14.99
VOL. 112 – QUEEN	00701052 / $16.99
VOL. 113 – JIM CROCE	00701058 / $16.99
VOL. 114 – BON JOVI	00701060 / $16.99
VOL. 115 – JOHNNY CASH	00701070 / $16.99
VOL. 116 – THE VENTURES	00701124 / $16.99
VOL. 117 – BRAD PAISLEY	00701224 / $16.99
VOL. 118 – ERIC JOHNSON	00701353 / $16.99
VOL. 119 – AC/DC CLASSICS	00701356 / $17.99
VOL. 120 – PROGRESSIVE ROCK	00701457 / $14.99
VOL. 121 – U2	00701508 / $16.99
VOL. 122 – CROSBY, STILLS & NASH	00701610 / $16.99
VOL. 123 – LENNON & MCCARTNEY ACOUSTIC	00701614 / $16.99
VOL. 125 – JEFF BECK	00701687 / $16.99
VOL. 126 – BOB MARLEY	00701701 / $16.99
VOL. 127 – 1970S ROCK	00701739 / $16.99
VOL. 128 – 1960S ROCK	00701740 / $14.99
VOL. 129 – MEGADETH	00701741 / $16.99
VOL. 130 – IRON MAIDEN	00701742 / $17.99
VOL. 131 – 1990S ROCK	00701743 / $14.99
VOL. 132 – COUNTRY ROCK	00701757 / $15.99
VOL. 133 – TAYLOR SWIFT	00701894 / $16.99
VOL. 134 – AVENGED SEVENFOLD	00701906 / $16.99
VOL. 135 – MINOR BLUES	00151350 / $17.99
VOL. 136 – GUITAR THEMES	00701922 / $14.99

VOL. 137 – IRISH TUNES	00701966 / $15.99
VOL. 138 – BLUEGRASS CLASSICS	00701967 / $16.99
VOL. 139 – GARY MOORE	00702370 / $16.99
VOL. 140 – MORE STEVIE RAY VAUGHAN	00702396 / $17.99
VOL. 141 – ACOUSTIC HITS	00702401 / $16.99
VOL. 142 – GEORGE HARRISON	00237697 / $17.99
VOL. 143 – SLASH	00702425 / $19.99
VOL. 144 – DJANGO REINHARDT	00702531 / $16.99
VOL. 145 – DEF LEPPARD	00702532 / $17.99
VOL. 146 – ROBERT JOHNSON	00702533 / $16.99
VOL. 147 – SIMON & GARFUNKEL	14041591 / $16.99
VOL. 148 – BOB DYLAN	14041592 / $16.99
VOL. 149 – AC/DC HITS	14041593 / $17.99
VOL. 150 – ZAKK WYLDE	02501717 / $16.99
VOL. 151 – J.S. BACH	02501730 / $16.99
VOL. 152 – JOE BONAMASSA	02501751 / $19.99
VOL. 153 – RED HOT CHILI PEPPERS	00702990 / $19.99
VOL. 155 – ERIC CLAPTON – FROM THE ALBUM UNPLUGGED	00703085 / $16.99
VOL. 156 – SLAYER	00703770 / $17.99
VOL. 157 – FLEETWOOD MAC	00101382 / $16.99
VOL. 159 – WES MONTGOMERY	00102593 / $19.99
VOL. 160 – T-BONE WALKER	00102641 / $16.99
VOL. 161 – THE EAGLES – ACOUSTIC	00102659 / $17.99
VOL. 162 – THE EAGLES HITS	00102667 / $17.99
VOL. 163 – PANTERA	00103036 / $17.99
VOL. 164 – VAN HALEN 1986-1995	00110270 / $17.99
VOL. 165 – GREEN DAY	00210343 / $17.99
VOL. 166 – MODERN BLUES	00700764 / $16.99
VOL. 167 – DREAM THEATER	00111938 / $24.99
VOL. 168 – KISS	00113421 / $16.99
VOL. 169 – TAYLOR SWIFT	00115982 / $16.99
VOL. 170 – THREE DAYS GRACE	00117337 / $16.99
VOL. 171 – JAMES BROWN	00117420 / $16.99
VOL. 172 – THE DOOBIE BROTHERS	00119670 / $16.99
VOL. 173 – TRANS-SIBERIAN ORCHESTRA	00119907 / $19.99
VOL. 174 – SCORPIONS	00122119 / $16.99
VOL. 175 – MICHAEL SCHENKER	00122127 / $16.99
VOL. 176 – BLUES BREAKERS WITH JOHN MAYALL & ERIC CLAPTON	00122132 / $19.99
VOL. 177 – ALBERT KING	00123271 / $16.99
VOL. 178 – JASON MRAZ	00124165 / $17.99
VOL. 179 – RAMONES	00127073 / $16.99
VOL. 180 – BRUNO MARS	00129706 / $16.99
VOL. 181 – JACK JOHNSON	00129854 / $16.99
VOL. 182 – SOUNDGARDEN	00138161 / $17.99
VOL. 183 – BUDDY GUY	00138240 / $17.99
VOL. 184 – KENNY WAYNE SHEPHERD	00138258 / $17.99
VOL. 185 – JOE SATRIANI	00139457 / $17.99
VOL. 186 – GRATEFUL DEAD	00139459 / $17.99
VOL. 187 – JOHN DENVER	00140839 / $17.99
VOL. 188 – MÖTLEY CRUE	00141145 / $17.99
VOL. 189 – JOHN MAYER	00144350 / $17.99
VOL. 191 – PINK FLOYD CLASSICS	00146164 / $17.99
VOL. 192 – JUDAS PRIEST	00151352 / $17.99
VOL. 195 – METALLICA: 1983-1988	00234291 / $19.99

Prices, contents, and availability subject to change without notice.

Complete song lists available online.

www.halleonard.com

0618